CRYSTAL HEALING

BEGINNERS GUIDE TO 30 BEST HEALING CRYSTALS TO KNOW AND USE FOR BALANCE, CLARITY AND RELAXATION

Disclaimer

Disclaimer and Terms of Use: Effort has been made to ensure that the information in this book is accurate and complete, however, the author and the publisher do not warrant the accuracy of the information, text and graphics contained within the book due to the rapidly changing nature of science, research, known and unknown facts and internet. The Author and the publisher do not hold any responsibility for errors, omissions or contrary interpretation of the subject matter herein. This book is presented solely for motivational and informational purposes only.

Table of Contents

Introduction 5

How Do Crystals Come to Be? 10

The History of How Crystals Were Used Throughout Time 15

The Therapeutic Benefits of Crystals 22

Your Chakras and Crystals: A Powerful Combination 29

Crystal Grids: The Benefit of One and How to Set it Up 39

Shopping for Crystals: What You Should Know 43

Using Crystals: 53

Understanding Your Emotional and Physical Responses 53

Profiles of 30 Crystals for Healing, Balance and Clarity 57

Conclusion 88

Introduction

For as long as our world has existed, precious gemstones and crystals have been a part of it, drawing attention to the person who was fortunate enough to find it. They couldn't help but admire its beauty and the colors that those natural materials had—so beautiful and unique, nothing else like it in the world. And people, living in an unprocessed and non-digitally stimulated world sensed the magical and mystical abilities of these crystals as soon as they held them.

Imagine having a clear mind, very aware and in the present. It seems wonderful, doesn't it? Then imagine what could happen if you picked up a beautiful gemstone that you found and discovered that it helped to give you the energy or awareness to solve a problem, perhaps made you feel better if your health was not what you'd liked. That's how crystals and gemstones become so revered in days long ago. Today, people are becoming more aware of the benefits that semiprecious stones hold for healing, the reduction of stress, and overall relaxation and clarity of the mind.

This book is an act of love that I have put together for you; one to share my experiences with crystals and give you the information you need to know so you can start using them for holistic, better health, both mentally and physically. Our bodies are of this earth and when we remove the obstacles in our way, whether made by others or our own frames of mind, we can really see where we are challenged, struggling, or blocked. On the positive side, we can find our strengths, opportunities, and the gifts that we have to make ourselves better and the lives better of those around us.

It's exciting to share with you all the information you need to really get the basics of crystals, including:

- Learning about how crystals are actually formed in the earth, as their source is a part of your quest for solutions
- Some history on how crystals were used over time and throughout our world
- Information on the therapeutic benefits of crystals
- The science behind how crystals work
- Where all your chakras are and how these wonderful spots within your body can be used in conjunction with crystals for powerful results
- What a Crystal Grid is, how to create one, and how to use it to its fullest potential
- Advice and wisdom on shopping for crystals
- The best ways to cleanse, charge, and program your crystals
- How crystals shift your emotional and physical responses, and how to understand these changes
- The profiles of 30 wonderful crystals that have potential to transform your life

All of this information has been put together with the intent to reach out to you and show you how small, simple steps that connect you with the earth's natural healing abilities can help you to have a more thriving, happy, and calm life.
There are so many ways that we can help ourselves become balanced individuals who have greater clarity and focus in our lives. One of the best ways to do this is by incorporating a ritual that involves gemstones, as this will help create an environment where they are a part of it. Life can grow and flourish and reveal its amazing potential when we let it; seeing firsthand how crystals lend to this vision is a loving and wise choice.

Regardless of how you choose to use this book, whether you take away a lot of ideas or a few, I feel confident that you'll latch on to information that leads you to a better feeling of wholeness, clarity, and strength. The changes may not happen overnight, but with mindfulness to your thoughts, emotions, and physical presence, you are giving yourself the ability to become more attuned to positive changes and energy in your body.

Enjoy your journey, my friends.

How Do Crystals Come to Be?

Often far below the surface of the earth where we can see what's happening, there is something occurring which is allowing the earth to give us wonderful gifts that we can eventually find when the time is right, these gifts are crystals.

Crystals all begin as minerals and form through a process that is called "nucleation". During this process they begin to grow through one of two ways:

Unassisted nucleation: starting with a single molecule

Assisted nucleation: through the help of existing solid matter

Nature decides which of these processes it will use when a crystal is born that comes from the earth, and not from man. Yes, you will want to pay attention to make sure you are purchasing authentic crystals, not synthetic reproductions. Because it is nature that gives crystals their ability to promote so much wellness in a person.

In order for any crystallization to occur, there are 5 things that must take place. It is the interaction between all these steps that lead to the final result—the beautiful crystal that we are drawn to as we seek out the best crystals for us.

First, the proper ingredients must be touching in some way. Not all combinations of ingredients—even natural ones—will lead to the formation of a crystal.

Second, the temperature must be favorable to spur on the onset of the process. As a standard, the warmer the temperature, the faster crystals form.

Third, there must be some type of natural pressurization that occurs to make the crystal start to take shape. For example, diamonds come from coal being tightly pressed together.

Fourth, time must pass in order for the crystal to form. We can all likely take a lesson about being patient with time the way nature does, because it is only through time that the true beauty of something is often exposed—especially a crystal.

Fifth, space is what comes last, as the crystal slowly separates itself from the place where it came. I like to think of that as the "womb" and the crystal is the child that has grown and flourished due to Mother Nature's loving care.

Through these five stages, the minerals that make up the initial “base” of the crystal will begin crystallization at a level that reflects the conditions it is found in. As mentioned, colder climates mean slower growth (which is okay) and the amount of space that the crystal has to grow is what will determine its size and how long the crystallization process takes.

It’s the movement of the magma underneath the earth’s crust that will determine what that temperature is and how the shifts occur that give the crystal what it needs to transform into what we will eventually see, hold, and gravitate toward for healing. Occasionally, the earth will shift in such a way that it isolates the crystal from being able to form, in which case, its matter will eventually start all over again in the crystallization process when its conditions are more ideal. I find that fascinating and a wonderful reminder of how our human spirit is not one to give up permanently, but just move on and start anew when its necessary.

When it comes to the color of crystals, it has to do with the minerals used to create it, as well as the chemical composition of the gemstone which creates the patterning, as well as the color. This is why there are so many variations in the colors of certain gemstones and we cannot assume that all Rubies or Jade or Turquoise are identical in color. These differences are what make gemstones so amazing, really, as they are beautiful works of art that occurs naturally.

On occasion, new materials make their way into a crystal, including fossils, which can actually lead to producing a beautiful crystal that has a fossil-like imprint on it. This is quite rare and amazing.

There are so many factors involved in making a crystal, none within our control as man, and that's why through our care and appreciation of our world, we can recognize how it creates wonderful things for us to use for making our lives better, in an authentic and holistic way.

The History of How Crystals Were Used Throughout Time

For as long as documented man has existed, a fascination with precious gemstones and crystals has existed, as well. The use of talismans—those artifacts with magical or healing powers—has been documented for centuries, along with the use of amulets. These earliest forms of using nature's gifts to create a better connection between man and mystery were mostly organic in nature, using the materials that the earth provided, such as ivory from Mammoths that were excavated in Russia to create beads, primarily.

Another item that was found frequently was Baltic Amber, some of it dating back over 30,000 years, which was discovered in the United Kingdom many thousands of years ago.

Regardless of where we live and exist, there is something about crystals and gemstones that draws our attention and makes them a part of our culture or life in some way, if not a part of history lessons that are passed down through the ages. Because of this, we are better able to intricately understand that there is a history behind their existence, and a person or group that understood and experienced their healing abilities in some way.

When we look through documented history, the earliest references to crystals came from the Ancient Sumerians, who also used crystals as a catalyst for their magic. And, as in most aspects of ancient history, the Egyptians showed a very involved relationship with crystals, using it in their jewelry, as well as understanding that there were ways to use the precious gemstones they uncovered for protection and health. They even used gemstones for make-up, by grinding them down to a powder that they used as eye shadow (called kohl). Today, we can be thankful that cosmetics are not made from crystals, but many of the shades we see are inspired by the beautiful, hard to replicate colors, of natural gemstones.

When it came to ancient Greece, a scientifically driven culture in many ways, they began to research the properties of crystals and named many of them—the names we know them by today are derivatives of these Greek words. The word "crystal" comes from the Greek word ice.

Once upon a time, they believed that clear crystal was ice that was frozen in the ground so deeply that it would always remain solid.

Through ancient Greece's studies, we also saw the onset of very specific rituals in which people used crystals for specific purposes. Amethysts were worn to prevent drunkenness and hangovers. Hematite, an iron ore crystal, was rubbed over soldiers bodies for protection before they went to combat. These are just two of many examples of these practices, all with specific purpose and intent, just like what we have today when we use crystals.

The one precious gemstone that is most associated with a certain region is Jade. We always think of ancient China with this stone and how it represents their spiritual beliefs, as well as a significant part of their art and culture itself. Some things which were made from Jade include: musical instruments, burial face masks, statues, carvings, and beads. They also used Jade to help in healing and treating conditions of the kidney. Other cultures used Jade to make pendants which represented their ancestor spirits. These pendants were passed down from generation to generation—imagine how wonderful it would be to receive such a treasure today. Today, countries such as New Zealand have traditions involving green stones because of the luck they bring. And of course, we cannot forget Ireland when it comes to associating green with good fortunes and merriment.

All known religions have ties to crystal and gemstones, as well, in some way. They are mentioned in holy writings, such as the Bible and Koran (and many others). In fact, it is through religion, and the breastplate of Aaron, a High Priest that is mentioned in the book of Exodus that birthstones were originated. In Hinduism, the Kalpa Tree is used to symbolize offerings to the gods and it is said to be made entirely of precious stones. There are mentions of diamond thrones used for meditation and harmony. It's endless, but one thing is clear, man has always valued what nature has provided in the way of beautiful gemstones and crystals—gravitating toward them, then being drawn to revealing their full potential through the use of their chosen spiritual practices.

And as time went on and centuries past, the Renaissance period began and the medical aspects of gemstones began to really take flight. There was this intense curiosity about how they could combine gemstones with herbal remedies to treat certain ailments. It drew the attention of many who were excited to explore this fascinating concept, but not everyone was happy about such research, especially some in power or a place of religious authority. You see, there was a time when it was believed that gemstones were sources of evil, corrupted by the sins of Adam.

Today, gemstones are not used medicinally in "traditional" type medical settings, but there are more people that are gravitating toward them because of the desire to seek out different ways to heal the heart, mind, soul, and physical self.

Others admire gemstones for their beauty and find them lovely visual reminders of the beauty that our world has in it, naturally made and wonderful to observe. Whatever you choose to do with crystals in your life, one thing is sure—you are creating your own history with them and allowing them to assist you just by their very presence.

The Therapeutic Benefits of Crystals

Many people are first introduced to crystals through holistic rooted healing methods, such as Reiki, for example. That draws interest and in turn, that draws research, which leads people to find out that crystals and gemstones do have a proven method of helping in healing, health, and wellness for those who use them properly and make them a part of their daily life rituals.

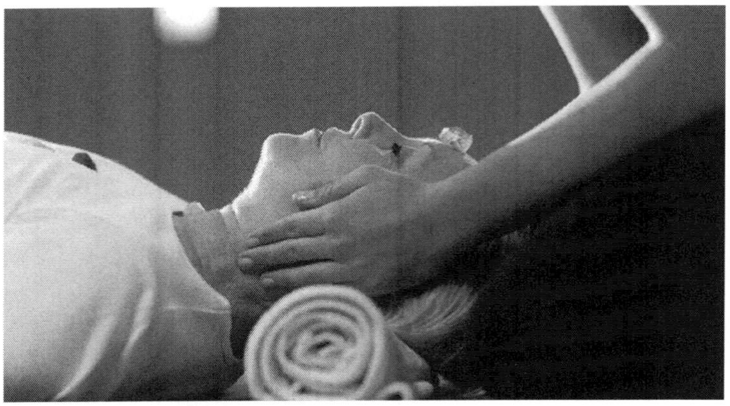

Today, as more people recognize the life that exists within crystals and precious gemstones, they become more aligned with how these wonderful gifts of the earth can help them to be more aligned with the universe and at a higher vibrational level within it—the higher the vibrational level, the more wonderful the rewards.

Colors have meanings and this is in large part due to items such as crystals, as certain colors typically offer certain benefits, whether it is for physical or emotional healing and wellbeing. Out of the many thousands of crystals out there in this world—many that we may never see or even discover—there are a certain few that we are aware of that can help us. This is a great color guide for you to use if you're seeking out specific solutions to concerns or problems that may be ailing your physical or spiritual self.

Red crystals are what we use when we are in need of stimulation or energy. This may be due to restless sleep, having the proper mindset for something big and significant in our lives, or because we are operating slowly and need to create balance.

With pink crystals, we use them to help find resolutions to the concerns that we may have. They help to extract our emotions and sensitivities in our daily actions, offering calmness and reassurance while doing so. When we are dealing with suppressed emotions (which can lead to physical problems, as well) pink crystals are wonderful to help us gently allow those emotions to surface.

Orange crystals give us energy and the ability to better focus. This allows us to unblock mental setbacks or even blockages within our body that can create problems for us. And if we think of orange as the sun we can visualize how powerful it is at helping us absorb wonderful feelings, with orange crystals and gemstones, they help our body absorb vitamins and minerals that lead us to better nutrition and healthy blood flow and circulation.

By using yellow crystals, we can help ease our nervous and digestive systems, while strengthening our immune systems. Through this, we are able to find happiness and contentment, while reducing fear.

Green crystals are associated with life, and in specific, the heart—both the physical and emotional heart. Our emotions and relationships are more harmonious and loving through these crystals. With our physical heart, we can find the gifts of stress reduction and decreasing of anxiety to help us be kinder to our physical selves, therefore our emotional selves, too.

With light or aqua blue crystals, we are able to connect with our throat and open up our communication channels better, as well as our sight, smell, and even taste. By expressing ourselves better, we are encouraging stronger emotional wellbeing, as well as an ability to explain what we are experiencing in life, whether it is a problem within us or a problem we have with the world around us.

Indigo crystals are linked to understanding and intuition, which can help us to be proactive in all aspects of our lives. What they help us to reveal are most often things that can help us grow in some way, or move on from something that has been holding us back.

By using violet crystals, we can find our inspiration, empathy, imagination, and even how we can better serve others. Violet brings balance and helps to eradicate the extremes that we may be experiencing from emotions or our physical state. When we are able to find peace and harmony within us, many times we can see what's really going on—the clutter and chaos is removed.

White and clear crystals have the unique ability of being able to reflect all the energy that is around them, which is a way to detoxify our minds and offer ourselves the gift of clarity. Working closely with "universal energy", these crystals can take in what we need and retract what is holding us back.

When we use black crystals, we are absorbing the light and all the energies around us, which is how we are better able to see the hidden potential of the situations we are encountering in life, whether by choice or happenstance. With black crystals, patience becomes a part of our strategy, as we know that we can figure things out over time and many times, the answers we need are not immediate, they come with time and a willingness to seek them out.

Therapeutic properties exist in almost everything we find in nature, in some form, but it is through crystals that we can give ourselves access to a sustainable source of goodness that will not get worn out or fade with time. There is no limit as to how many times we can use crystals to help offer healing to ourselves in some way, which makes them ideal for not just one time solutions, but also for chronic physical and emotional conditions.

Your Chakras and Crystals: A Powerful Combination

Chakra is a Sanskrit word that means wheel or disk. Our bodies have seven main chakras that are referenced, sometimes by number and other times by name. With each of these chakras there is an alignment with the spine, which starts at the base of the spine and works its way up to the crown of our head.

The reason that it's important to pay attention to our chakras is because they contain bundles of nerves and major organs, and play a major role in our spiritual, emotional, and psychological health. Our goal is to always have our chakras:

- **Stay open**
- **Stay aligned**
- **Stay fluid**

When there is a blockage in our chakra, energy cannot flow and this is what often stops us from being at a place of optimal health and wellbeing, many times without us knowing it. Things get congested and toxic activity takes place. Think of a clogged bath drain—it's unappealing and you can see how it isn't working properly. Our chakras are much the same way—when they are blocked they cannot work and communicate properly with the rest of the body, which leads to problems.

Awareness it the single most important first step one can take to keep their chakras open. The task of doing so may not always be easy, but it is possible with the proper balance of crystals to help promote the process, along with taking the time to recognize that you are a wonderful being in this world with needs that matter and need to be fulfilled.

Here's an example to show what we mean: a woman has recently lost her child and is grief stricken. As a result, she develops bronchitis, which lingers in her chest, not wanting to heal and creating great pain and discomfort every time she coughs. In this case, her heart chakra is what is impacted. By seeing the connection between her loss and the sickness, she can promote healing and move on, while still honoring the grieving process and physical treatment to the ailment.

1. **Root Chakra:** the first Chakra is responsible for stability, security, and meeting our basic needs. When this chakra is open we recognize a sense of safety and feel fearless. Coral, Bloodstone, Garnets, and Rubies are wonderful gemstones to use in conjunction with this.

2. **Sacral Chakra:** the second Chakra is aligned with our creativity and sexual center. It's located above our pubic bone and below the navel. Aventurine, Ruby, Carnelian, and

Citrone are gemstones to pay attention to if you are concerned about this area.

3. **Solar Plexus:** this is the area from the navel to the breastbone and our source of personal power. We draw energy from this Third Chakra and it is very connected to our vitality. Citrine, Calcite, and Topaz are gemstones to seek out if you have concerns with this chakra.

4. **Heart Chakra:** the fourth Chakra is where we connect the spiritual with matter. Located at the heart's center, this is the middle of all the chakras and the place where energy flows and is transferred throughout the entire body. Aventurine, Jade, Rose Quartz, Kunzite, and Rhodochrosite are gemstones that are interesting to take note of if you feel that you are having concerns or blockages that stem from the heart.

5. **Throat Chakra:** the fifth Chakra is located in the area of our throat and is the place where we need to have openness in order to communicate both verbally, being mindful of our highest truth. The neck, thyroid, parathyroid glands, tongue, mouth, and jaw are also a part of this chakra. Lapis Lazuli, Turquoise, Kyanite, Blue Topaz, and Azurite are crystals that are helpful in opening up the throat chakra.

6. **Third Eye:** this sixth Chakra is located between the eyebrows and is the center of our intuition. This is something that we all have, but little use, which can lead to blockages that impact our lives in more ways than we know. By clearing this chakra we can begin a relationship with our intuition and the valuable wisdom it carries for us in our lives. Amethyst, Moonstone, and Sugilite are crystals that you should use to help address concerns of the sixth chakra.

7. **Crown Chakra:** the seventh Chakra is located at the crown of the head and is the one that guides us to enlightenment and a spiritual connection with our higher selves, others, and the universe as a whole. By obtaining this greater state of self, we are able to bring together our lives as a whole, creating harmony and unison through awareness of something more in this universe than just ourselves. Diamonds, Herkimer Diamonds, and Clear Quartz are the crystals you want to use to help open up this chakra.

Through the seven chakras, we are able to create an alignment within us that works for both our emotional and physical wellbeing, changing our perspectives and often our course of action to one that is for the better. We can see that the decisions we make to be better for ourselves are never ones that harm others, but in fact help, as when we are whole, we can inspire others to greater action, as well.

When your chakras are out of balance you will sense this, because everything seems more chaotic and there is a constant fluctuation between balance and disruption. Some examples of both emotional and physical imbalance would be:

- **First Chakra:** loneliness, insecurities, feeling ungrounded, unconfident, abandoned, indecisive, depressed, anxious, addictions, phobias, obsessions / lower-back pain, sciatica, varicose veins, constipation, diarrhea, rectal/anal problems, impotence, water retention, and problems with groin, hips, legs, knees, calves, ankles, and feet

- **Second Chakra:** eating disorders, addictions, low self-confidence, dependency issues, low libido, and unbalanced emotions / kidney problems and urinary tract infections, chronic lower back pain, sexual disorders, infertility, gynecological problems, dysfunctional menstrual cycles, and problems with the intestines, spleen, and gallbladder

- **Third Chakra:** lack of memory and concentration, frequent fearing, feeling un-centered, sugar addictions, insomnia, and eating disorders / digestive and intestinal disorders, indigestion, food allergies, eating disorders, poor metabolism, diabetes, obesity, eczema, acne, and other stress-related skin conditions

- **Fourth Chakra:** apathetic, faithlessness, unforgiving, hopelessness, distrustful, uncommitted, and detached / pneumonia, asthma, breast problems, respiratory problems, upper-back pain, shoulder and upper-arm pain, and premature aging

- **Fifth Chakra:** nervousness, anxiety, fear, attention deficit disorders, poor coping skills, feeling isolated / problems with the nasal area, irritated sinuses, sore throat, jaw pain and TMJ, voice loss, thyroid problems, teeth and gum problems, and ailments of the esophagus and tonsils

- **Sixth Chakra:** headaches and migraines, nightmares, seizures, neurological disorders, personality disorders and neuroses, learning difficulties, and hallucinations / eye problems, glaucoma, ear problems and hearing difficulties, spinal conditions, and scalp/hair issues.

- **Seventh Chakra:** depression, confusion, loss of faith, mentally disconnected, dementia, epilepsy, schizophrenia / light sensitivity, headaches, dementia, autoimmune disorders, neurological disorders

By healing the chakras through the use of crystals and other holistic means of offering ourselves better love and health, we can often circumvent problems that lead us down the paths of drugs, costly doctor's appointments, and other options such as that. Of course, if you have significant problems that concern you seeking out a medical experts' advice is recommended. Using crystals in conjunction with what they may suggest is a smart idea, as well.

Crystal Grids: The Benefit of One and How to Set it Up

A crystal grid is not unlike a dream or vision board. It's a powerful, spiritually energized tool that you can use to help manifest what you wish for to come true. Perhaps it's that ideal relationship or maybe a new career or financial freedom—regardless, it has a better chance of coming to be your reality if you give it the mindful attention it deserves, using the crystals that can help it to manifest.

The benefits of using a grid compared to an individual stone for this comes from the cohesive way that different crystals work together to energize and create for the specific intent you have. The geometric patterns that make up a grid will help you to be aware of what you desire, as well as increase your focus on doing what is necessary to manifest these desires.

In order to get started, this is what you will need:

- The place in your home or office where you'd like to put your crystal grid—think of natural lighting and places that you find peace or tranquility at whenever possible.
- To have your intention or goal written out on a small piece of paper.
- A distinctly different crystal for the center—one that appeals to you or perhaps a crystal point that directs your grid up to the universe (it's a powerful image).
- The gemstones that have qualities that will help your vision.
- A quartz, which is what is used to activate the grid.
- A cloth made of natural materials, or perhaps a crystal grid cloth if you have access to one.

Once you have everything you will need ready, this is what you will do next to create your crystal grid:

1. Clean the space you will be placing your crystal grid by burning sage over it or breathing in slowly, clearing the air around you through your own energy to purify the area.

2. Fold your intention that you wrote out and place it in the center of the cloth.

3. Breathe in deeply and state your intention out loud. To make this step more powerful visualize it into existence at the same time.

4. Place your center crystal that you chose on top of the intention that you folded and placed in the center of the cloth.

5. Take your quartz crystal point and then begin the lay-out of all the gemstones for your grid. You can make it whatever pattern you wish, but the most effective and beautiful ones are like a connect-the-dots in a way. I have found great success

> when I think of how I visualize a chakra—a swirling pinwheel pattern when I create a crystal grid.

This is what it takes to create your crystal grid. You may want to surround it with candles or essential oils, or something else that provides a fragrant reminder to keep manifesting your hopes in your mind and believing that they will come to be. Because it's a wonderful moment—that moment when you realize that what you've hoped for has come into existence in your life.

Shopping for Crystals: What You Should Know

When shopping for crystals you have several places that you can find them, including: online retailers, holistic health shops, and shops that specialize in authentic gems and minerals. Any of these options are acceptable, but you will want to make sure that there are a few things that you are receiving with your purchase, because certain gemstones can be costly. They will only be worth that price if they are as you believe they are.

- Make sure the crystals and gemstones are authentic

- Instructions on cleaning and powering the gemstone should be with all purchases of authentic healing gemstones

- The properties that the crystal is known for should be available to you

- The individual or onsite retailer you work with should be reputable in gemstones and their benefits; and through reviews you should see evidence of their knowledge and their credibility

In addition to these tips for making the most of your purchase, you should also consider the spiritual side of you purchasing a crystal. Some of the most exciting things you may find when you are deciding to purchase (especially in a store) are:

- A specific gemstone that just appeals to you for some reason (it doesn't even have to be clearly defined, but there is a reason—investigate it).

- Don't feel you need to purchase an entire set of gemstones at once that will fit every single need you may sense you have. Buy a few at a time so you are not overwhelmed and make sure you use them the proper way, as you'll be sure to notice the difference. Plus, a few adjustments in one area can lead to improvements in another area.

- Have an idea of what is troubling you before you go look to purchase; this can send out great energy to attract you and the right gemstones for your situation to each other.

Crystal Care: Cleaning, Charging, and Programming

Gemstones are the most effective when you take the proper care to clean them. By doing this, you are clearing them of any energy they may have picked up during your previous use of them that would make them not as effective. Since you are using them for healing, stress relief, and relaxation, it's important to treat them with care so they work better for you. There's no better way to experience their full benefits and properties.

There are many ways in which you can clean your gemstones, some working better for certain stones. Whenever you purchase a stone you'll want to make sure to follow the recommended instructions. Don't worry—these are processes that are easy to do and don't take a lot of time. I find that the process of cleaning and recharging stones is one that is quite relaxing to me, an act of love, if you will, from me to them in gratitude for how they help me every day.

You may be wondering why you can't just clean a gemstone in one specific manner or why they need to be cleaned at all, but there is a good reason for it. Every gemstone is as unique as every human is. Some of them are fantastic after just an hour of sunlight, while others will fade and lose their properties by too much exposure to the sun (Amethyst, for example). Likewise, some stones will actually dissolve in water, whereas others are rejuvenated from being submersed in it. You really just need to double check and any reputable gemstones seller will have instructions that help you take the best care possible of the crystals you choose to purchase from them.

Here's a list of some of the most popular ways to cleanse crystals and recharge them so they are at their best for your needs.

Energizing cleansing: you can use either the sunlight or the moonlight for this. With moonlight, there are a few options but you must be more mindful of them, as it does require a daily reminder to do it and many times. With the moon you can choose either a full moon or moonlight cleansing over a longer period of time.

- For a full moon—place the crystals in a clay pottery dish and cover them with water (from the ocean if possible) and then leave them there until the morning. You'll awake to crystals with a beautiful new energy to them.

- For moonlight cleansing—this may take several hours or days; you'll want to expose the stones to all the moon phases, placing them outside every night at dusk and then retrieving before sunrise.

Water cleansing: if you're fortunate to be near an ocean, you can use the ocean water to cleanse the crystals; however, if you do not have access to fresh ocean water you can use a bowl of salt water or water from a natural water reservoir, such as a lake, river, or pond. Other options that are wonderful with water include:

- Scrub your crystals with either a cotton cloth or natural loofah under cold tap water

- Use Love Energy Waters, which is something you can either make or purchase. This process incorporates spiritual harmony with the actual cleansing process, making it a relaxing and loving process.

- Sea water is another way to energize and cleanse stones. Going to the beach and making this a ritual that feels wonderful under the sun and with the cool sea water splashing on your legs is invigorating for the body and the soul.

- Rain showers—a natural, refreshing, and wonderful way to cleanse and reenergize stones. Also a wonderful chance to bring out that youthful innocence that you still have if you choose to dance and enjoy the rain while cleansing your crystals.

- Hold crystals under warm running water and take a moment to be mindful of the feel, sight, and sound of this. A wonderful experience!

Incense and herb cleansing: by smudging your crystals with incense and herbs such as lavender, sage, sweetgrass, frankincense, etc. you are making the process more spiritual and intentional, which can be quite good for your psyche, as well as your appreciation for the situations you are addressing in your life with the crystals. This is a wonderful process that can be done in conjunction with moon, sun, or water cleansing.

Cleansing with Selenite: this crystal is the universal stone cleanser, as it is not only helpful and therapeutic for healing, but also cleanses other stones. If you set your stones on the Selenite you can cleanse them that way. For added power, just like many methods, you can add the full moon, cleanse inside or outside, or even set them in the sunshine (if the gemstone will not be compromised in the sun).

Other favorite cleansing methods: there are wonderful ways to create harmony by bringing together the earth's most natural, spiritual, and cleansing ingredients with the crystals that you are using to help create more awareness and positive, energetic changes in your emotional and physical health. Consider some of these effective, loving cleansing ideas:

- Purify crystals in a bowl of brown rice overnight

- Bury crystals in the earth for a more ritual purification—salt of the earth, so to speak
- Use Reiki methods to cleanse and energize crystals
- Use Breath of Intention ritual. Blow three exhales over your crystals, while visualizing positive thoughts and holding them
- Imagine pure white light shining down on your crystals, closing your eyes and visualizing pureness and goodness—the positive energy in your thoughts and body will help in the cleansing

Hopefully you're excited about all the great options that are available to you for cleaning your gemstones. There's a method for everyone and a way to maximize the impact of every crystal you choose to have.

Using Crystals:

Understanding Your Emotional and Physical Responses

Through the use of crystals, you will begin to notice changes, some subtle and some clear. Being aware that this is normal—and healthy—is going to help you through the process and understand what is happening better.

On the physical side, you want to:

- Make sure you drink plenty of water or herbal teas—natural ingredients that keep you hydrated as your body and mind begin to transform, clear chakras, and heal
- Eat natural foods as much as possible, as unprocessed foods will help to clear up your mental and physical energy, giving you the proper nutrition to maximize the benefits of the crystals
- A more relaxed body with fewer stress points

- A sounder night's sleep
- The need to catch up on sleep, as your body needs more energy to heal

On the emotional side, you are going to experience a change in how you may normally process things around you, including:

- More awareness of your emotions as they begin to take form
- A greater call to more immediate action based on your gut instincts
- Releasing of painful emotions such as sorrow, anger, grief, and anxiety
- Bursts of euphoria as you begin balancing out your emotional scale
- Great confidence in your choices and decisions
- A stronger sense of empathy, while not giving out your energy to others and making their problems yours
- The ability to listen better, as your internal chaos will calm down

- The ability to communicate more clearly, as you will not have the blocks that stop you from speaking concisely from your heart and mind

The points mentioned above are good for you and are also a few of the more common responses that crystal users have found over time. In general, this newfound awareness is a liberation of the heart, mind, and soul, leading you to a place of enlightenment where the impossible is now possible. The scary is now glorious and full of wonder. But best of all, your ability to appreciate and live the moment can thrive as a result.

Profiles of 30 Crystals for Healing, Balance and Clarity

There are many crystals out there to choose from, but here is the top 30 that I believe you will find tremendous value in as you begin to explore this wonderful way to become more whole. Take advantage of that abundance of positive energy that can flow through you with the proper care and attention to "non-traditional" approaches to a better you.

Alexandrite: Associated with prosperity, this stone changes colors, which makes it quite unique. If you are looking to win at something or increase your luck, having Alexandrite by you is suggested, as it will help generate the positive energies that help in your success. It also offers courage. Alexandrite is associated with promoting better circulation and stronger blood vessels as well, which are good for overall health.

**Use with the second chakra*

Amazonite: Known for bringing out truth, self-love, clarity, patience, trust, and tolerance, Amazonite is ideal for those who are about to present big ideas and artists who wish to make a statement in their expression. It's known for relieving blocks that hinder and hold one back in some way. For health, this crystal is beneficial in helping the body absorb calcium, which is beneficial for the bones, teeth, muscle spasms, and menstrual cramps, as well.

**Use with the throat and heart chakra*

Amethyst: Amethyst offers clarity of thought, relief from grief, and also protection and wisdom. Through this crystal, you can find a wonderful offering for yourself or a friend who is in mourning, menopausal, or going through life changes that disrupt their rest. Through its powerful properties, the amethyst is able to calm the soul and bring clarity to the mind, which works wonderfully for stress relief, alleviating negative emotions, and creating the motivation to work through problems. Amethyst also balances hormones and strengthens the immune system, and is good to use for healing blood related problems and diseases of the lung.

**Use with the third chakra*

Amber: This is a very popular option for babies and young children, as it helps to calm and sooth, while also lessening pain that can come from teething or ear infections. For many, using Amber as a talisman for prevention is something that they do, finding that it promotes a more relaxed and positive thought process with less worry. Amber is wonderful for cleansing impurities also.

**Use with the solar plexus chakra*

Black Tourmaline: What is wonderful about this stone is that it can be used for all kinds of protection and it also shields you from unwanted or unhealthy energy. This means that if there was ever one stone that you'd want to carry with you every day or have access to, it would be this one. This includes helping with all of your emotional and health concerns, as well.

**Use with all the chakras*

Blue Topaz: Known for bringing good fortune, better communication, wisdom, honestly, forgiveness, and abundance. For health, it is a wonderful crystal to aid in digestion while balancing the nerves and stimulating metabolism. Use this crystal if you or someone you know is a creative person, such as a writer or artist, or there is a need to apologize for something.

**Use with the fifth chakra*

Carnelian: A stone that is filled with vitality and life force, its energizing presence is ideal for anyone who is feeling lethargic or drained, whether it is due to health or the pace of their lives. It brings about the balance and moderation that is necessary, making it a wonderful stone to have nearby as you take on new projects or adventures. Carnelian also promotes better sexuality and strength.

**Use with the root and sacral chakras*

Citrine: Many are drawn to Citrine, as its properties include appealing things such as prosperity, courage, strength, joy of life, protection, and open mindedness. Entrepreneurs and students, in particular, are quite drawn to this crystal because of how it can energize you on all levels. It aids in better decision making and optimism, while improving concentration and intuition. For health, it is a wonderful addition to bring balance and harmony to stressful emotional situations, which tend to hold one back.

**Use with the solar plexus chakra*

Crystal Quartz: A wonderful crystal that promotes calmness, clarity, healing, harmony, and energy. Crystal Quartz is a perfect gift for yourself or someone who may have to work at a computer all day or that is having a problem relaxing. This is one of the best crystals one can use for purifying the sprit, mind, and physical body.

**Use with the crown chakra*

Flourite: This gem can come in many colors and is wonderful for helping one to guard against negative energy, making it very helpful for those who are addressing volatile situations or relationships. It helps to dispel anger and eliminate the haziness that stops one from having clarity, which reduces stress and brings about more positive energy.

**Use with the crown chakra*

Girasol: This is a wonderful gem to have available if you are striving to become more creative, find unique and new solutions to problems, and also improve your ability to be able to tap into your dreams and remember them better. Physically, if you suffer from diseases such as diabetes, chronic fatigue, or have problems with your metabolism, Girasol can help to manage those symptoms and offer comfort and relief.

**Use with the crown and third eye chakras*

Hematite: This stone helps people find a sense of stability and feel more grounded, making it ideal for people who have put too much on their to-do lists and find themselves struggling. It also offers a sense of comfort to one who has it on them, bringing them security in who they are and what they are approach. Having this near you for job interviews is a wonderful way to encourage a balanced and wonderful experience. Hematite is also beneficial for healing negative energies that impact muscle tightness, the head, and posture.

**Use with the root chakra*

Herderite: A stone to help you discover new pathways to solutions that perplex you, this is an ideal stone for people to use when they are making big decisions that will impact the flow of their life, bringing them more confidence as they go through their process. It brings harmony and unity to your freewill and spirit, helping guide you to the better choices. It is also wonderful for clearing channels inside through promoting better circulation and the ability to breathe in deeper and self-rejuvenate.

**Use this with the crown chakra*

Herkimer Diamond: This high vibration gem will help open up positive connections with the universe to find the answers you seek and to experience the world around you in greater clarity. It's ideal for those who feel as if they've lost themselves through taking care of others needs and ignoring their own. Herkimer Diamonds are also wonderful gems to use for promoting a stronger immune system to keep sickness at bay and your energy levels up.

**Use with the crown and third eye chakras*

Jade: With Jade, we can gain acceptance for things that may challenge us in some way, whether it is accepting the impact of another's decision or coming to terms with a decision we must make that's long overdue. It gives us the inner harmony and calming energy to be gentler with ourselves and less critical, while doing what is best for us from a place of compassion. When it comes to longevity in life, Jade is the stone that most turn to.

**Use with the heart chakra*

Kyanite: This blue crystal is exceptional at facilitating communication with guides and angels, opening up a pathway to understand and recognition. Due to its balancing properties, it is wonderful at helping to align the chakras when they are not in alignment. Use Kyanite if you have problems with your eyes, headaches, or other struggles that drain you of energy and the ability to communicate well.

**Use with all the chakras*

Lapis: This gemstone is fantastic for those who wish to solve a pressing problem or discover why they have reoccurring, strong emotions that they don't understand. Its ability to help unblock the answers and solve the mysteries makes it very valuable. When it comes to physical wellbeing, Lapis is effective in treating the throat and alleviating symptoms from sickness.

**Use with the third eye or throat chakras*

Malachite: If you long to find love and prosperity, this is the gem for you. It will help you to find greater self-acceptance and positive energy that will draw these things to you. It helps to balance your thoughts and increase your magnetism so the things you desire find their way toward you. Malachite is also beneficial to those who suffer from prolonged grief, depression, and low stamina.

**Use with the base chakra*

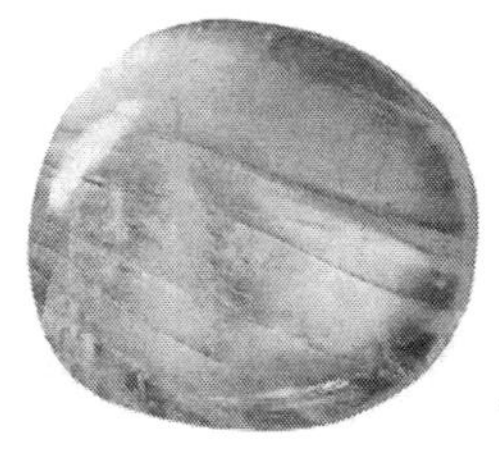

Moonstone: Moonstone is a wonderful crystal for moms-to-be or new mothers, as its properties promote love, happiness, feminine energies, and psychic abilities. This stone is very associated with new beginnings, success in love and business, as well as good fortune. It's also said to perceive what "is", which makes it a very personal stone. Moonstone also helps in balancing the digestive system, absorbing nutrients, and lessening the presence of toxins in the body.

**Use with the crown chakra*

Nebula Stone: This stone is one of the most powerful out there for removing negative forces and influences from inside the body, whether they are in the mind or soul. For people who are struggling with identity problems or severe emotional duress, they can find assistance through this stone. When it comes to struggles with vitality and stamina, or problems of the kidney, this stone is the one to use to regain control and energy.

**Use with the base chakra*

Obsidian: This is a grounding and protecting stone, which makes it a wonderful stone to have if you are going to be traveling or embarking on a new adventure that you are uncertain of. It helps one to recognize that they can make decisions in that moment and need not be held back by things in the past. This brings about serenity and clarity that make all changes more calming and logical. If you suffer from infections, whether chronic or acute, Obsidian can help to lessen those symptoms.

**Use with the base or third eye chakra*

Onyx: With properties that offer support, strength, stamina, and protection, people can find a wonderful crystal to help in their lives when they are in a period of transition. Onyx has the ability to help manage stress and challenging situations and also gives us intuition and assists with good fortune. Health-wise, if you suffer from skin ailments, infections, or inflammation, consider using this stone to help with those conditions. As a word of caution, this is a stone that needs to be cleaned and recharged more frequently than some others.

**Use with the base chakra*

Pearl: The Pearl is a gem that is easy to find and has wonderful benefits for women, in particular, including soothing affects for infertility and female-related health problems. It is also valuable in aligning one's self with prosperity, wealth, and success.

**Use with the crown chakra*

Pyrite: A wonderful stone such as this promotes creativity and offers protection, greater intellect, and intuitive powers. Someone who may be starting to network more or rely on others for business or creating social networks should keep this stone close, as it will help them be more aware of the individual. For those who have blood and circulation systems, using Pyrite to promote better flow is a smart idea.

**Use with the third eye and base chakras*

Rose Quartz: When you want to experience love, regardless if it is romantic, self love, platonic love, or even unconditional love, or enter into a state of deep compassion and caring, you want to look to Rose Quartz. This makes it the perfect crystal to use for those who are broken hearted, lonely, and also for pregnant women. Known as the "heart stone" to many, Rose Quartz is also known for strengthening the physical heart by stimulating circulatory systems.

**Use with the heart chakra*

Ruby: A gem that represents vitality, energy, zest and zeal, love, healing, passion, and courage, the Ruby is an essential for those who struggle with insecurity and depression. It assists with releasing destructive emotions and patterns so we can love ourselves better, while also inspiring passion and a resilient life-force. For better health, the Ruby is exceptional for those who need/desire a cleansing and detoxifying of their body, as well as their lymph system.

**Use with the sacral chakra*

Sapphire: Money, protection, and communication are what draws so many to this gem. Through its use, people are better able to remain calm and connect with the things they desire and often work so hard for. If you know of anyone graduating from school a gift of sapphire is a wonderful idea. When it comes to your health, Sapphire helps to decrease inflammation and fight off fevers.

**Use with the throat chakra*

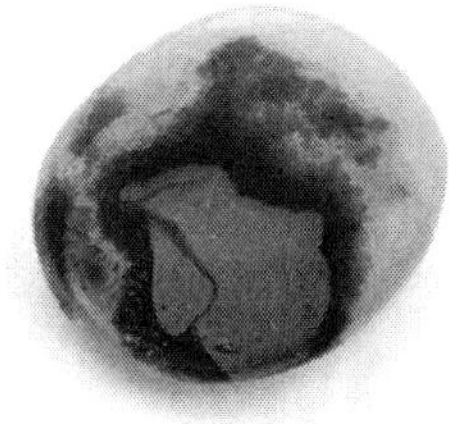

Septarian: When it comes to dealing with things that we tend to hold onto, despite it being time to let go, Septarian can assist in the process, guiding one to a new perspective that will help in the process, whether it's forgiveness or acceptance that's needed. When it comes to health, Septarian can be used to nurture old wounds and alleviate discomforts that they may inflict upon someone.

**Use with all chakras*

Turquoise: This is a crystal that is known for wonderful properties that include protection, wisdom, positive thoughts, friendship, courage, and balance. Giving or receiving turquoise is a wonderful gift for someone who speaks frequently in public forums or is having relationship issues. Turquoise is also well known for its healing powers and ability to draw disease out of the body and strengthens female energy, helping in conditions specific to women, and also soothing headaches.

**Use with the throat chakra*

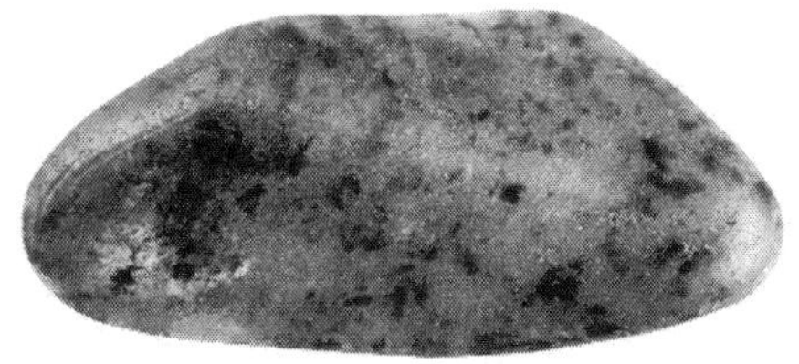

Zoisite: Promoting universal love without fear, this is a wonderful stone to offer those who work in service to others or do volunteer work, especially overseas. It helps to bring out their true intentions. Zoisite is also a powerful stone to use for those who suffer from adrenal or circulatory system problems that impact how they operate within a given day.

**Use with the heart chakra*

Conclusion

As you go to sleep tonight, take note of what is weighing you down and how you feel. If there is something that is off balance, it's time to use all the valuable information you learned in this book and seek out a solution. At the same time, the universe in its loving way will help those solutions come to you. Together, you and gemstones have the ability to change the world one person at a time—starting with you, the place where all your answers and solutions lie.

Printed in Great Britain
by Amazon